This Is Not Shakespeare

RICHARD LOVEDAY

BookLeaf Publishing

Presentation by *BookLeaf Publishing*

Web: www.bookleafpub.com

E-mail: info@bookleafpub.com

ISBN: 9789357213455

First edition 2023

I dedicate this book to anyone who feels like a fraud.

I dedicate this book to anyone who is unable to see the good in them that they see in others.

I dedicate this book to anyone who feels like they are not enough.

You are strong. You are beautiful.

You are enough.

Bottom line is, even if you see them coming, you're not ready for the big moments.
No one asks for their life to change. Not really. But it does. So what are we, helpless? Puppets?
No, the big moments are gonna come. You can't help that. It's what you do afterwards that counts.

That's when you find out who you are.

Whistler
Buffy The Vampire Slayer
"Becoming Part 1"
Season 2, Episode 21

I Am An Imposter.

Maybe that's a bit dramatic, I really am Richard, sometimes known as Richie, Chardy Balls, PT, Rich T or The Mr Messy. It all depends on how we came to speak. Or how I came to avoid your direct gaze.

Here's a little secret: I don't know who I am. There a whole list of things which I am not which include, but are not limited to the following:

- Funny
- Good at singing
- Likeable
- Talented
- Athletic
- Masculine
- Sexy
- A writer
- Popular
- Normal

These aren't self-deprecating 'woe is me, i have it hard' observations. No, these are things I have been made aware of during the 32 years I have inhabited this mortal coil.

I am also not Shakespeare. Clearly. I was not born in Stratford-Upon-Avon during the reign of Queen Elizabeth the 1st. I did not marry Anne Hathaway (not Catwoman). and have never been referred to as 'Bard' (unless someone is describing my karaoke prowess or I have caught a cold). I have not written a single play, never mind had anything I have produced described as the finest of anything. I am not quotable, I am not studied in classrooms all over the world, I am not the inspiration behind Hollywood movies.

I am lucky to be surrounded by people who don't seem too bothered by things that I'm not. They like (or tolerate) me for what I am. Which is..

I don't exactly know. I don't really fit in anywhere, not in a 'lone wolf, I work better by myself and will save the president' kind of way. Between the depression and anxiety and major imposter syndrome, I have never really fit in.

Following the release (shameless plug) of my first collection of poems, 'The Little Black Book' in 2021, I took some time to understand myself; I'd done the grieving that follows a breakup, the realization that I was able to move on and that I was ok by myself. [This isn't going to turn into a story about washing up on a desert shore, and fighting tigers until able to escape on a raft I built with the aid of my volleyball friend. I am also aware that I am not Tom Hanks.].

I just didn't have a true sense of who this 'self' was. It was a throw away conversation (which the person probably won't remember) that challenged me to push myself; I imitated the style of the great Bard, tried styles I had no place being involved with and, Lord above, even took a detour back to God.

Ol' BIlly Shakes is the standard, the bar I have compared myself to; Romeo and Juliet, King Lear, Midsummer Nights Dream, Hamlet, Macbeth… These are some of the works that impacted me growing up and inspired me to want to be 'a writer'. (I also blame him for my desire to find the other player 'of my star crossed lover' storyline).

The following pages are the result of the 'exploration' into uncharted territory. There's love. There's loss. There's betrayal. all the makings of a Shakespeare play, but without the finesse or body count of a Shakespeare play.

And lists. A lot of lists, as I pick out all of the things that I am not in order to find out what, who, where and why I am.

No, this is not Shakespeare.

But I look forward to finding out who it is.

Previously…

Alnilam.

Is this peace?
Maybe.
How sad to discover that my 'free' came at a price;
an Asterix.
1,051200 tarnished moments
Where lonely wasn't alone.
In a crowd,
In a hall of memories where we hide behind smiles?
Each smile waiting.
Waiting?
For relief?
An escape.

Realization sinks in;
I tried to hold the sand together
1,051,200 grains
In a relic where the cracks shredded
Shredded my fingertips.
You watched me keep together,
Try to hold a useless trinket
Watching,
Lonely but not alone,
As my palms would scar and bleed.

But can this now be peace?
The quiet roar of silt,
1,051,200 individual abrasive particles
Tarnishing the surface of my soul.
Each moment.
Each memory.
Buffeted by coarse grains.
Lonely.
But not alone.

Those finger prints;
All that remains
The only evidence
That you once held my heart.
In the cold you set it down
Beneath the flakes
1,051,200
Chilling my heart.
Lonely but not alone.
This terminal disease.

Under a suffocating quilt of bleak
I leave my toxic dreams.
I remain a sickle,
Moving into incurable
To remission to believe
That lonely and now alone
We suffer apart.

1,051,200 seconds.
Carcinogenic
The poison.
The we no longer stuck or spit
Now willing to see
That to remove limb to save the body
Was perchance the best way to proceed.

I took the steps.
1,051,200 to be exact.
Mine the only footprints in the sand.
I find peace here like a mirage,
Feel the ripples.
Feel the sifting sands.
The dust seeps from my soul,
No fissure lay beneath
As the cracks being to smooth.
Lonely but not alone.

So here I lay,
In a sea unburdened by debris.
No mourning in the East,
No sun set in the West.
I let the darkness wash over me,
I lay beneath a sheet of black.
1,051,200 sparks of twilight meet my eyes,
And the night resets my soul.
I let the darkness upon me,
While Orion's Belt fastens together

The collective shards
Of my damaged heart.
Alas we find peace?
Perchance?
Alive and now aware:
That alone is no longer lonely.

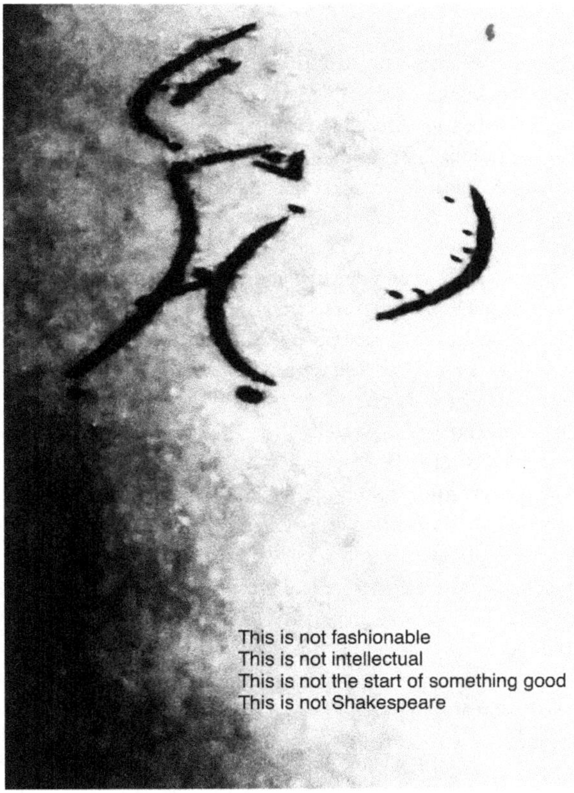

This is not fashionable
This is not intellectual
This is not the start of something good
This is not Shakespeare

Capture The Flag: Across The Valley

A man leans against a flag pole, one warm summer evening, drowsily reading the pages of a mind long passed, when he catches the sight of a black bird flying above. Circling the mountain top, getting closer to the flag pole until it brushes against the tattered sigile high above the man's head. Reaching for the paper in the blackbirds beak, he read the words aloud.

'I've seen your flag across the valley, and while I have remained isolated for some time I wish to pass my kindest wishes for I recognise the standard of a cloth not unlike my own - The Red Queen'

The man responded in kind, sending to the Red Queen the poetry inspired by the valley expanse he called home.A day later the blackbird returned. And the day after. And the day after, continuing the exchange, until an understanding of sorts was reached.

'I have seen in your words a heart that could match my own. See here, the picture of my pennant and consider how they might stand beside each other? - The Red Queen'.

The man responded, explaining that, while he was happy to remain upon his mountain, he would consider the journey across the harsh valley floors if she could guarantee his safety.

'My friend, I write not of false promises. I shall meet you at the Milkwoods, and your loyalty shall be matched - The Red Queen'.

The man packs his pennant, and begins the descent from his refuge…

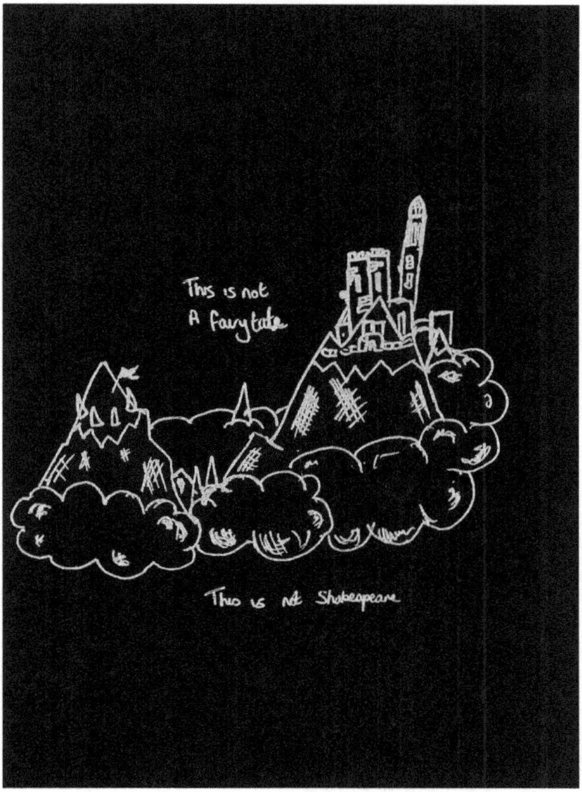
This is not
A fairytale
This is not Shakespeare

Scene 1

- ***Summer evening.***
- ***A well decorated kitchen/lounge.***
- ***'Human' By Aquillo plays in the background.***
- ***Sunlight streams through the windows.***
- ***Two men discuss their hobbies over coffee.***

1.M Well, it's just something that happened. It started off as a way to survive, pulling threads from the bundle of thoughts up here *taps head* and here we are. I have a book of poems coming out.

2.M But isn't that exciting?

1.M It is; I always wanted to write a book, I have a few stories there somewhere, I just don't believe it's something that will actually happen.

2.M Why is that?

1.M it feels too easy. Things like this never actually come off. And it's not like Iexpect anything to come from it. It's not really any good, it's not exactly Shakespeare.

2.M **Scoff** Well, neither was Shakespeare! In fact, most of his ideas came from Plato

Warm Bread.

Since I was young, on Christmas morn, my mam
Would start the day of festive definition
Making breakfast of boiled and roast smoke ham
Bucks fizz and cheese, a long running tradition.
Older, no magic could achieve the goal:
Raise me from slumber or drag me from bed
Better than the thought of those fancy rolls
Or the comforting smell of fresh baked bread.
This scent which reminds me of the good times
Excitement, happiness and family joy:
Softness and warmth shown with careful cut
lines
Each Christmas morning since I was a boy.

But you look at me and all I can say
Your smile is like warm bread, whatever the day.

This is not

- ◯ Fate
- ◯ Luck
- ◯ Karma
- ◯ Shakespeare

Crumbs.

When I think I'm ok, that I can be strong,
I see your face in a picture; that smile.
Those lyrical eyes which held me in song
Break me again, cutting through my denial.

I thought I could live on those crumbs, in hope,
But those same goddamn crumbs make me
choke.

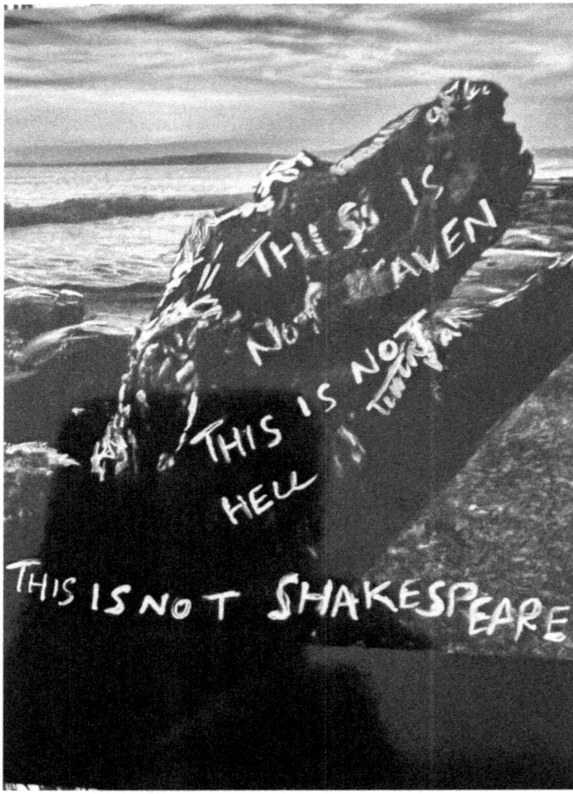
THIS IS
THIS IS NOT
THIS
HELL
THIS IS NOT SHAKESPEARE

Alice.

I truly hope that you find peace at night
And can close those eyes to escape your dark,
That you keep the horizon in your sights:
The closure that will reignite your spark.
So that from your pen excellence can flow
And the entire world will know your story
In my hands I'll hold a part of a soul
And feel the warmth of your splendid glory.
For now I'm out here; alone in the cold
Lips still tingling from the last time we touched
Pondering the worth of a 'Heart of gold'
Convinced it's not enough but still too much.
For you it may be a Wonderland past
But it seems I'll stay trapped in the looking
glass.

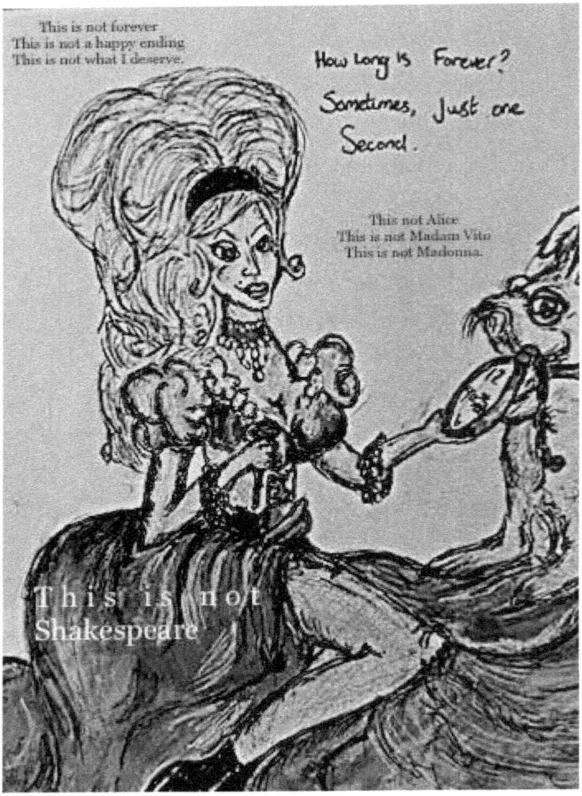
This is not forever
This is not a happy ending
This is not what I deserve.
How Long is Forever?
Sometimes, Just one Second.
This not Alice
This is not Madam Vito
This is not Madonna.
This is not Shakespeare

Burn.

Sometimes the thought of
Those freshly baked rolls
Is better than the feeling
Of getting your fingers burned.

Truly;
You've burned me deep.

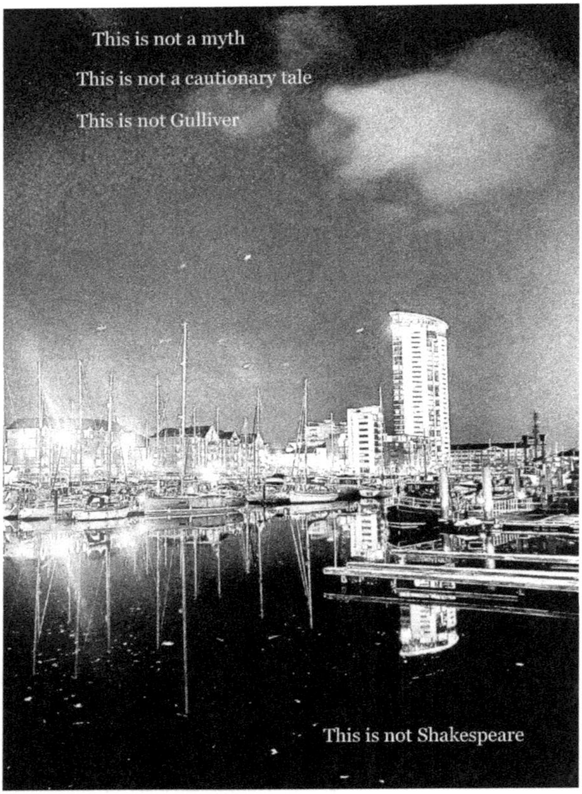
This is not a myth
This is not a cautionary tale
This is not Gulliver
This is not Shakespeare

Capture The Flag: Before The Red Queen

A man approaches a summit on a cool Autumn evening, when something bright and gold catches his eye. Before him, between the miles and miles of white roses stood a figure: The Red Queen, her crown polished to a blinding shine.

He followed the path created by thorny bushes, and stopped short of this impressive figure. A breeze carried fallen petals, like a cyclone of snow between them. The Red Queen smiled and the man recognised, that while she wore a circlet of auric splendor, it was the sapphires beneath her brow that cast bright against the setting sun.

The man responded in kind, taking to his knee with his head bowed; the journey had not been kind, but his strength returned with vigor in her presence. Before The Red Queen, raising his arms, resting there on his bloodied palms, he presented her his greatest treasure.

A pennant, patched and stitched, folded neatly to display a deep crimson heart.

The Red Queen kissed her finger tips, and placed her hand on his cheek, lifting his face to meet her gaze.

'If you can traverse the valley floora nd climb back from the depths of the dark you have true courage.

'If you can face the sunlight and not shy away from the glare, you have true strength.'

'If you can bow your head without concern for exposing your neck, you have true humility.'

'The path ahead is uncertain; the work I have yet to complete, from my previous alliances, and the legacy I have to protect, won't be easy. If you are to be my consort, you must understand.'

He kissed her hand. The Red Queen took the folded flag in her hands. Turned on her heels and walked towards her castle. The man followed.

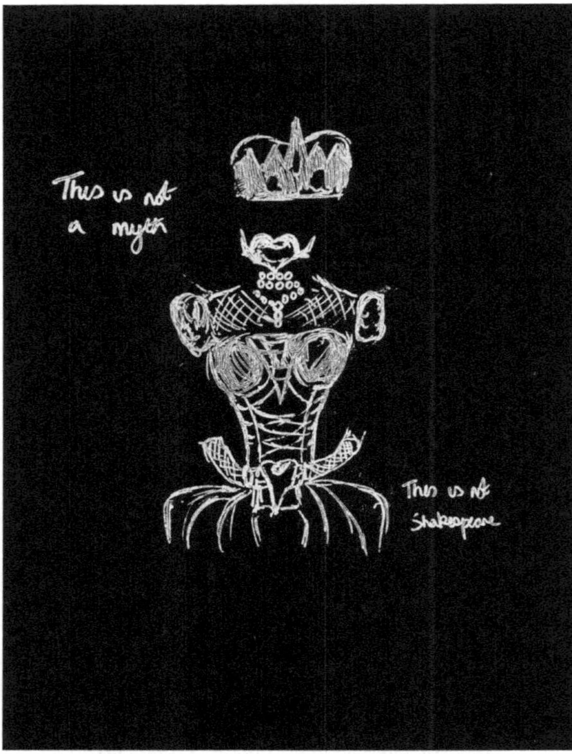
This is not
a myth
This is not
Shakespeare

Hope.

With the words you spoke forging promise in me;
The first rays of light to break through the dark
Underneath the door, a crack let me see
A long forgotten path we could embark.
I Admit to the fear of following my heart,
But you found me when I needed to hide
Within pages and threads I wove like art
And made it safe to lay by your side.
Ignoring the voices that begged to walk away
From a gamble that cost more than just luck
On someone who, face to face couldn't say,
What he found was too much and not enough.
Maybe hopes dagger is not mine to wield:
It just cuts through my palms should I dare believe.

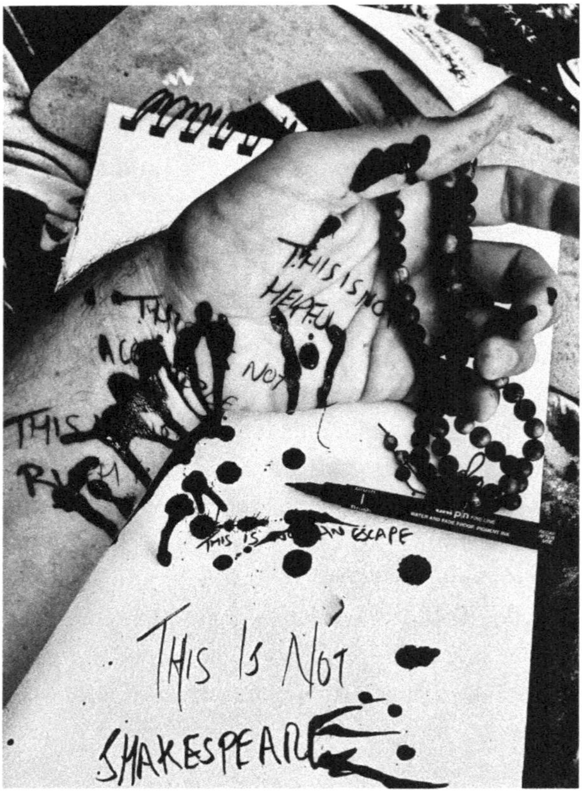
THIS IS NOT
SHAKESPEARE

Ssalg Gnikool Eht Hguorht Snoitcelfer.

He could not imagine what came to pass
As he watched the world through the looking
glass:

Dropping words to float on radio waves,
But glass bottles break through the calm surface
Drowning truth in depths on a salted page
By a current that held no true purpose.
How did calls to the night, buried in sands
Through the lunacy of the Mad Hatter,
Find their way from far shores into the hands
Of the one reader that truly mattered?
The shock of what he found made him spit tea
Beside the wall of the suited place;
Wonderland, once insipid to see,
Made vivid by the return of Alice!

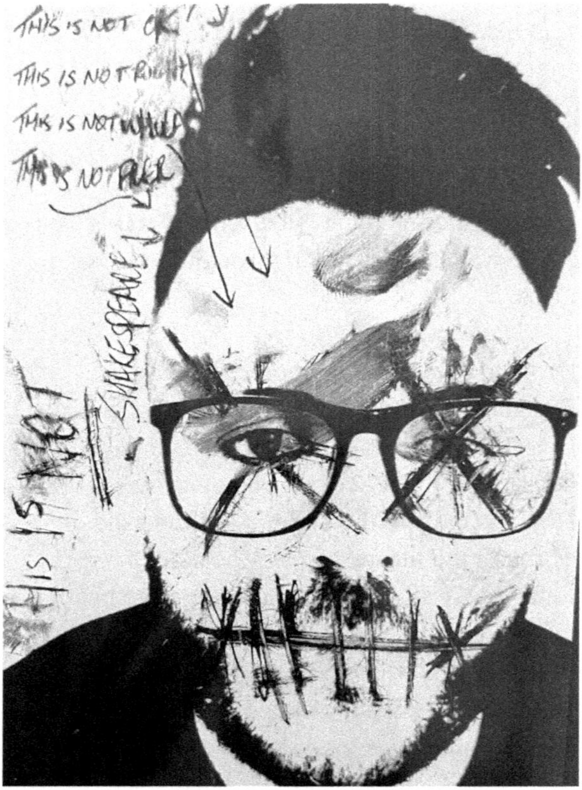
THIS IS NOT OK
THIS IS NOT RIGHT
SHAKESPEARE
THIS IS NOT

Falling.

I feel the force of gravity
But I'm barely down to earth;
High in the sky I feel like I'm falling,
Endless and complete.
I took a chance at flying without wings
But now plummet through the twilight air
You strip the feathers and draw me in
Truly. Madly. Deeply.

It's funny how you became a life raft
Dragging me out to sea;
Forcing me through torrential waves and fierce currents
That threatened from underneath.
I'm falling hard against the shore
On an island yet uncharted
And the soothing sound of the sea calms my fears
As I look upon the sunrise.

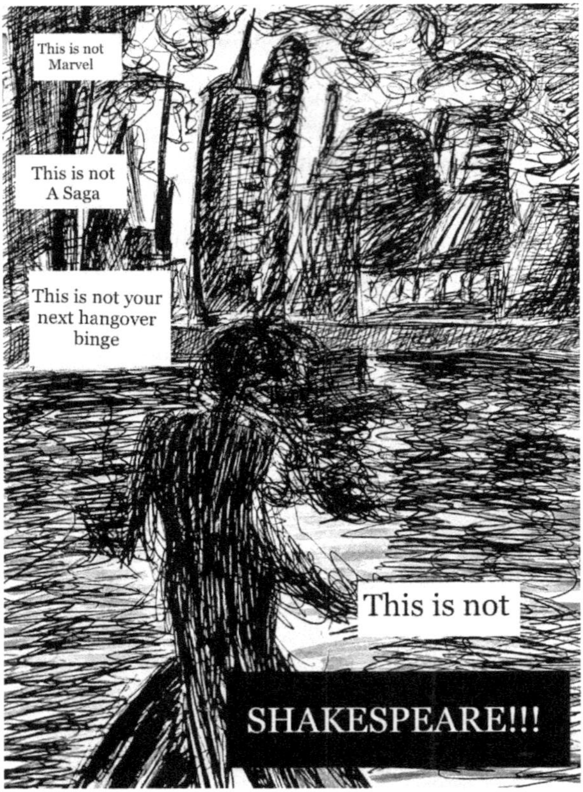
This is not
Marvel
This is not
A Saga
This is not your
next hangover
binge
This is not
SHAKESPEARE!!!

Scene 7

- ***Late Autumn evening.***
- ***A busy restaurant.***
- ***Plates are being cleared away.***
- ***Two men discuss literature over a bottle of rose.***

1.M I don't really know what to say. You actually put the work in. I literally just had a mental breakdown.

2.M Yes, you keep saying that but it's the passion behind it. It's raw and it's real.

1.M Yeah, I suppose. I mean, if someone reads it and it helps them to ask for help, you know the mental health thing… How about you? Why do you write?

2.M Because. It's the sort of thing I wish I could have read. When I was growing up, we were told stories. Everyone has a story that deserves to be told.

[Lights dim. Spotlight on the table.]

2.M I just hope my story helps someone understand their own story.

1.M ***[Voice Over]*** And it was then. The moment. He had me. Something about the words and the look in his eyes. And I knew. That was it.

[Lights Up]

2.M How do you feel about pudding?

Plain Text.

I've been used to burying my heart in lines
And weaving words to hide my thoughts in plain sight;
Hopes dressed up in themes and arranged in rhyme
Out of fear the truth would make you take flight.
Lifes too short not to say it, I'll be direct
But I never thought in you I would see
When I look back on the night we first met
Someone who made it safe an possible for me
To be open and honest strip back the allegory,
Break down my walls.
Write a new story
That starts as I fall…

Please forgive the lines you glanced above.
This cowards too scared to admit he's in…

This is not

- ◯ Another chapter
- ◯ Perfect
- ◯ A little black book
- ◯ To be noticed
- ◯ To be forgiven
- ◯ A Taylor Swift album
- ◯ For glory
- ◯ To heal
- ◯ How to raise Cthulu
- ◯ Easy
- ◯ Lyrical
- ◯ Polished
- ◯ Shakespeare

Capture The Flag: The Feast

There was a table set out under a rising sun, in front of a stained glass window that reached from the floor to the high arching ceiling of the great hall, and The Red Queen and the man were sitting at opposite ends of a long oak table . Flicking candles lined a runner positioned between them, and red roses climbed up the walls.

A grandfather clock ticked in one of the many rooms of the vast abode, echoing the chime to let the inhabitants know it was 6 am.

'I will be with you shortly,' The The Red Queen crooned, flag in her hand. 'Please, help yourself to coffee.'

The man picked up the white cup, the steam rolling over the brim and took a sip. He blinked.

The clock chimed 12 times.

The room was dark, and through the stain glass window, a crack of moonlight reached across the large table towards him. It can't be? It was just morning? He looked around; The roses had wilted, the candles had burnt out and he was alone in the room.

The Red Queen was nowhere to be seen.

The man pushed back on his chair to investigate; this was a peculiar situation. He waited, at the Red Queens request. And here he was alone. No table settings, no runner. Her throne was missing too.

And in her place sat a small black bottle.

The man walked the length of the room, and peered through the stained glass window. The moonlight breaking through the clouds revealed the ruins of a tower in the distance, but the man was sure shadows moved around the tower.

The man set out for the tower, convinced her the answers of what had happened must lay.

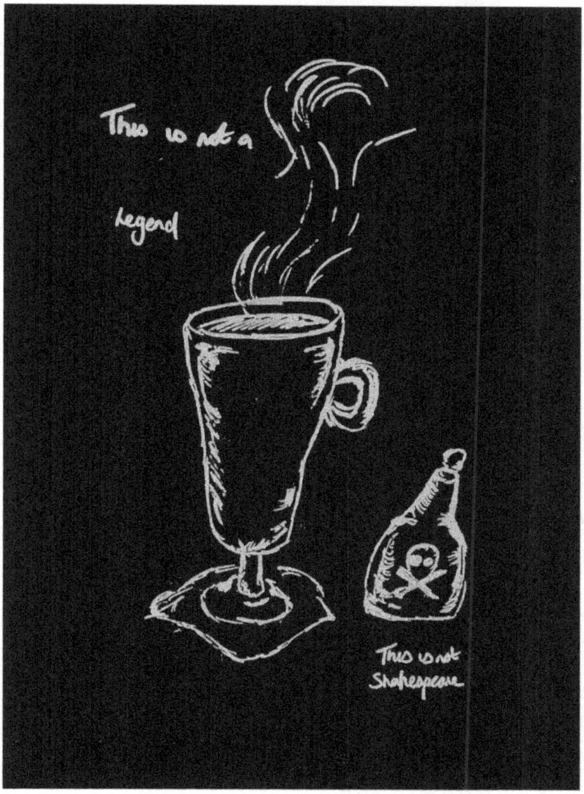
This is not a
legend
This is not
Shakespeare

A Prayer.

It’s been a while since I have prayed,
I can only say I’m sorry If I get this wrong.

I sit here in your home,
Full of questions I can’t answer
And it feels hopeless;
Can you guide me through the dark?
Father, Son, Holy Ghost,
Would you accept me
A lost lamb,
Back into your flock?
Ashamed,
I realize that I am jealous:
There are people, laughing and smiling,
Basking in your light.
They have belief, without proof
That they are safe in your love.
They have comfort
Knowing you are watching over them.
Are you there?
Are you watching me?
What is that,
To be so sure of your place in the world,
To know without knowing?
To see without seeing.

How is it possible?
The belief that there is a higher purpose,
To all the dark days
Terror,
Pain,
Seething loneliness…
How it can be just accepted
That to suffer is part of your plan,
That you don't give more than can be handled?
Am I handling it though?
Am I making you proud?
Was this part of your grand design,
For me to be broken?
I can't blame you that I would
Fall in with the devil.
And I fell. You saw, I fell.
Was this your punishment?
To be so filled with love for
Someone who would destroy me.
For turning my back from you?
I never understood how
How you created man in you image;
When you filled us with love, there was a
chance
Our love was wrong?
Is it possible to recognise someone
So corrupted?
I never chose to feel like this, I never
Chose to love this way.

The abuse, the hate, the anger
Not being accepted,
Being seen as less than.
Less that human,
Not worthy of happiness.
Is that how you feel?
Do you still love me?
Would you still love this abomination?
I'm kneeling before you
Asking for a chance
For clarity
For understanding.
For a way out.
I'm begging
Please, guide me back to the light,
I will follow your path
Please, show me compassion,
A compass out of purgatory.
I'm beaten.
I can't find it in myself.
I've lived in hell,
I live in hell,
I breathed, cried, endless nights awake
In a hell of my own making.
Give me a sign,
I couldn't be any farther from heaven,
But a sign, some acknowledgement
That I am not a lost cause,
Or broken,

Or worthless.
That I am still your child.
Can you forgive me?
Please, forgive me for who I am
For what I have become.
For the nights I blamed you for the pain,
The chaos,
The darkness that choked my heart.
Forgive that I became the waste of
Soul you see before you;
I have squandered my chances,
I have taken lightly
The gift you gave.
For the endless hours where
I longed to belong
And the twilight nights
Where I no longer wished to be.
Can I believe you?
Move from the cold,
To the light
At the end of the tunnel?
Will it lead me back to you?

Do you see me, for I can't see myself?

Are you there? Are you watching me?

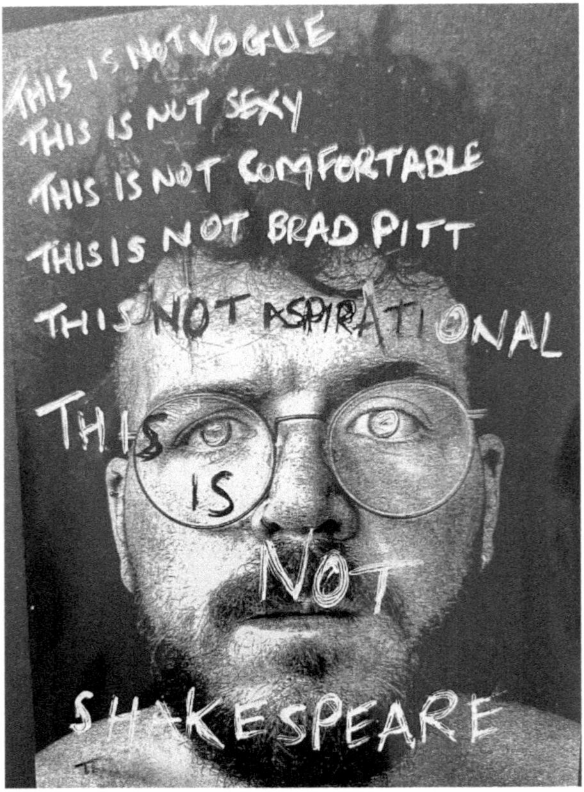
THIS IS NOT VOGUE
THIS IS NOT SEXY
THIS IS NOT COMFORTABLE
THIS IS NOT BRAD PITT
THIS NOT ASPIRATIONAL
THIS
IS
NOT
SHAKESPEARE

<u>Scene 12</u>

- ***Winter.***
- ***Carpark.***
- ***'All Too Well' by Taylor Swift plays in the distance.***
- ***It starts to rain.***
- ***Two men stand opposite each other.***

2.M I don't want you to wait..
1.M But I will. I am wa…
2.M Don't. Don't say that.
1.M No, don't. I will. I am . I have been. I won't say that word, not now it wouldn't be fair on you. But I do. I care. Deeply.
[Lights Dim. Spot light]
1.M ***[To the front of stage]*** It's there. That word. I look into his eyes and I see he's hurting and all I want to do is grab him, and kiss him and tell him it will be ok. That if I am everything he's looking for I can be everything he needs.
[Lights Up].
2.M You're everything. But I can't…

The Art of Bloom

Bouquet.
Simple stems,
Petals of pure white
Arranged In a vase on a table.
Pure of intent and loyal to a fault,
Fragile to the touch held in carved stone.
No sunlight, but a ray cuts through the grey day
Blooms passed from on hand to another
And you smile that smile,
I walk away; a single tear
Rolls down my cheek:
A single
Drop.

Arranged in a vase on a table.
Petals of Pure white.
Simple stems
A bouquet.

I wish I didn't understand
The art of bloom.

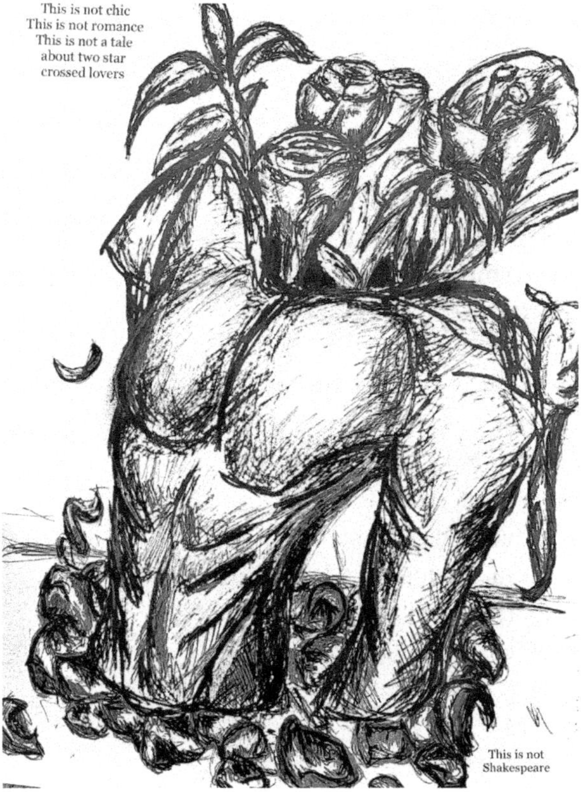
This is not chic
This is not romance
This is not a tale
about two star
crossed lovers
This is not
Shakespeare

Promise.

Miles.
Many a mile
that's been traveled,
yet so many more to go.
There will be a stumble, but
A hand will always be there to
Help pick you back up, guide you
Through a potholed wilderness
Where: hope seems to wane
And colds arms wrapped
Around you so tightly
It seems almost
Impossible to
breath.

Caves,
Caves atop a
Mountainous peak
Set aside from the living
Far away from civilization. You;
Retreating to a fortress of solitude
At times when storms get so loud, the
Thought of fighting drains you, pulls
What little strength you have left
Causes you to double guess

Your self worth, your value
In a world where time
is money.

So you sit
Alone in shadows
Shadows, wrapped in
A cocoon not of your own
Making. Nestled in a sadness
That almost seems tailored to your
Form. While there is comfort in the shadows,
And you will soon feel safe enough to
Venture out in the world, and be
Ready to face the day. That
Your fears and doubts are
Unfounded, that you
Will never be alone.

You have me.
It’s not much
But I will wait.

I promise.

32. This is not...

A. For us	B. For them
C. For you	C. Shakespeare

33. This is not...

A. About love	B. About anger
C. About hope	D. Shakespeare

Salt.

I turned back in the rain,
Step by step,
A punt, a shot.
A cliche engrained
As I confessed
That it was love, actually.

Is this my lot?

As I become a pillar
And dissolve into the night
I understand why
You should never look back.

To Be Kind.

No expectations.
Just a heart that
Shines in a
darkened room.

To be kind,
For no other need
Than to be,
Is a rare gift.

Flag:

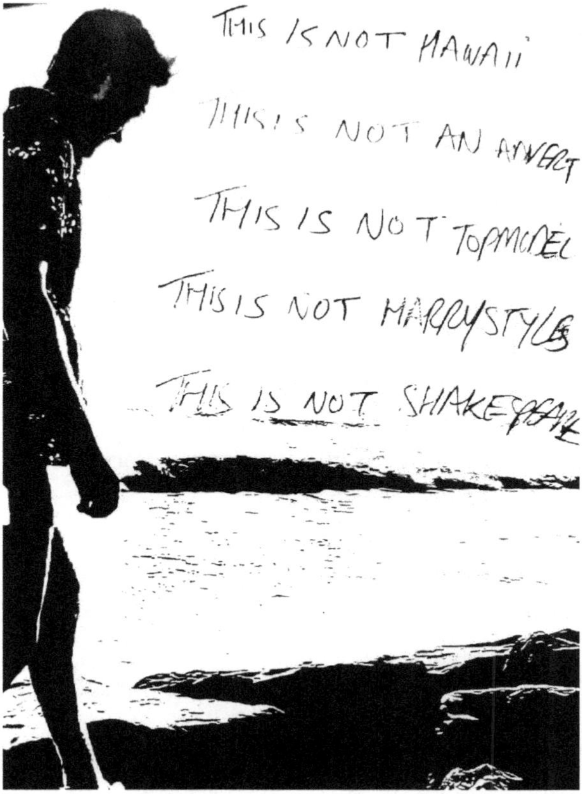
THIS IS NOT HAWAII
THIS IS NOT AN ADVERT
THIS IS NOT TOPMODEL
THIS IS NOT HARRYSTYLES
THIS IS NOT SHAKESPEARE

Walk Away.

When he's no longer the first to say good morning;
When there is no prayer for you sleep well a night;
Take it's as a sign,
There will be no warning.
Just as it's always tomorrow
And next week never comes;
No name on the page in your diary
But you're fingerprints all over my story.
If you identify the colours
In the pictures that I paint
Know it was your part in the narrative
That inspired this particular hue.

This is the last time I will convince himself
That I am is worthy,
Of the time or attention of someone who
Who wouldn't let me know you.
And the last time I looks at blooms,
In hope that for a moment
Your eyes would spark the light you hide
And show a future promise.
You weren't there,
You didn't care enough to care,

It wasn’t fair.
It was. Not. Fair.

Oh, a picture of perfection?
We are all human after all,
You collected up the pieces
Just to let this bastard fall.
To be swept aside and kept to hide,
To allow you to ignore that
I gave My heart, for you to disregard
The promise to just be there.
I tried to on keep going, to carry on regardless
To be pulled down in a way that was so
heartless;
You couldn't love, you wouldn't love,
You took my love and left me broken.

And the saddest truth of all?
The thing that hurts me deep?
I know that I'll come running back again
Should you decide to call.

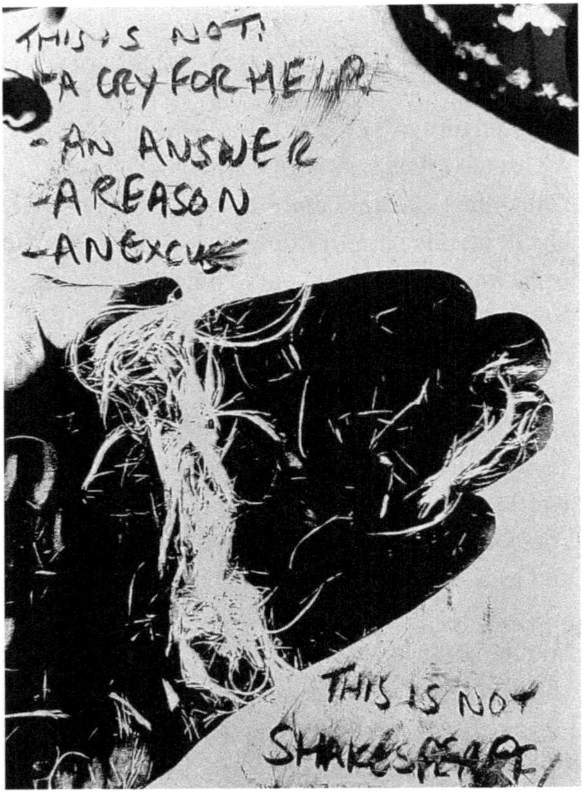
THIS IS NOT:
-A CRY FOR HELP
-AN ANSWER
-A REASON
-AN EXCUSE
THIS IS NOT
SHAKESPEARE

Capture The Flag: The Glass Jar

Through a crack in the door, hung at the top of a desolate tower, a dim glimmer trickled down the stone steps like quicksilver. Through broken windows, rain flooded the highest room of the castle and as he stepped inside, the man found the source of the waning light.

There, on a plinth, in the middle of the vast room, looking upon the vast cavern stood a glass jar. It took a moment for his eyes to adjust, but a wave of confusion and sadness enveloped him, as he realized, within the glass dome sat what once was his most treasured possession:

A pennant, patched and stitched, folded neatly to display a deep crimson heart.

The would-be suitor would recognise the remnants anywhere. Why, when gifted to The Red Queen who invited him within these walls, would she abandon such a precious symbol? In a peculiar fashion, The Red Queen had cast his standard aside while ensuring a level of protection that held his favor in limbo.

Time had carried on, faster than he was able to comprehend, but at the top of the tower, the man realized his token of love was kept far enough away that The Red Queen wouldn't be responsible for the welfare, but close enough to call on when loyalty is required.

This broke the man.

The Red Queen broke him.

And as lightning split the sky, the man hurled the glass jar to the floor, pushed the pieces to the side and picked up the folded flag. Tucking it beneath his shirt, the stitched remains of the tattered heart lay close to his left breast, as he descended the stone steps and back to the valley below.

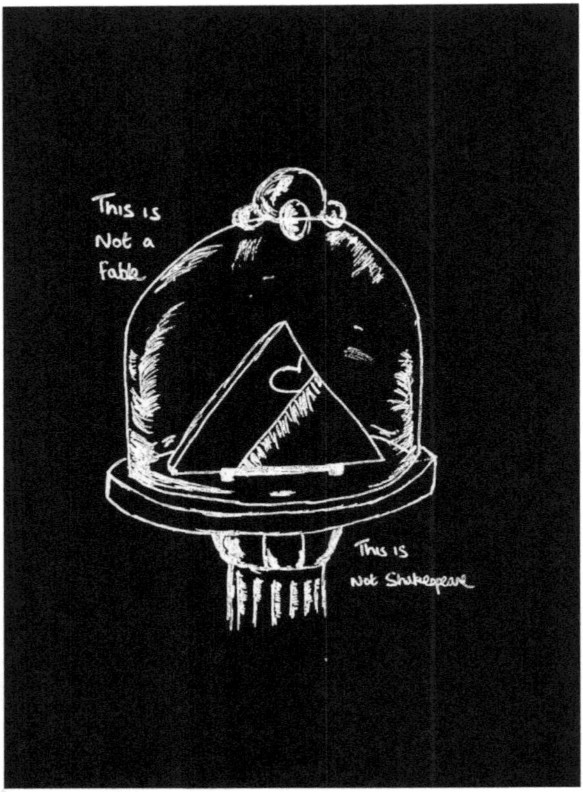
This is
Not a
Fable
This is
Not Shakespeare

The True Cost Of Sapphires

For three?

I traded my mind

Never understanding the debt
I would continue to pay;
How an aluminum oxide
- Set between pressured cut carbon -
In a band that mimicked forever
And skin torn by barbs,
Justify the fragmented shards left in my hands,
When it came to you whole.

For two?

I traded my heart.

Bruised and battle scarred,
I placed my love at your feet
For a future shining in azure iris
That foretold of pearls between
Between chaste smiles my hesitations slip away,
To loosen my fingertips and give my all
For the words that form on lips, building a world
Whose eyes would never see through?

For one?
I trade my soul.

The inky surface, broken in moonlight
Smash against the rocks in a siren song.
They call, the storm calls and I?
I bare my soul to the sea.
A jewel that gives and takes.
How I conmight barter,
Lingering along the shoreline,
To be dragged beneath the swell?

Nocturnal Requiem

You.
You echo through
The halls of my mind;
But I can't escape.
I thought I could run,
It's inevitable really?
I close my eyes, and
That sickness in my stomach
Rises up.
I can't scream,
I can't hide,
I can't breathe
And I am drowning in your presence.
You invade my sleep
With fear;

There is nowhere

I am safe.

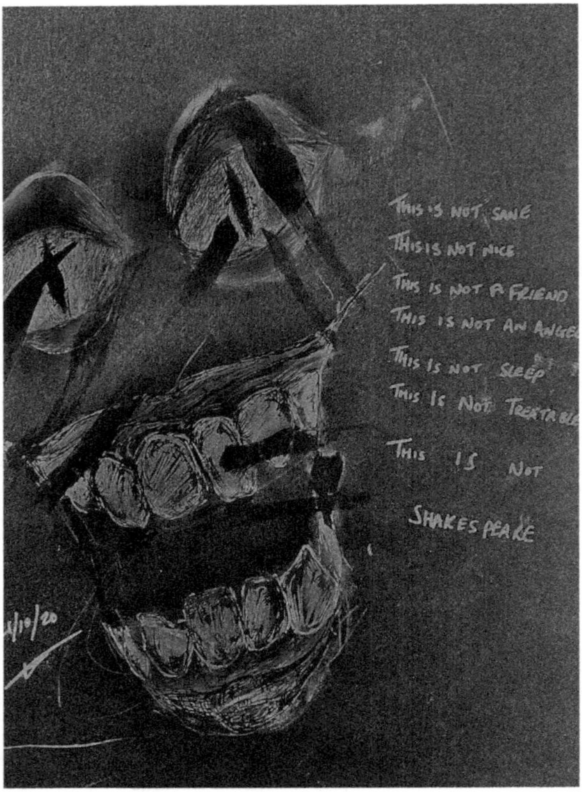
THIS IS NOT SANE
THIS IS NOT NICE
THIS IS NOT A FRIEND
THIS IS NOT AN ANGE
THIS IS NOT SLEEP
THIS IS NOT TREATABLE
THIS IS NOT
SHAKESPEARE

St Christopher.

Please guide me on my journey;
I have lost sight of my way home
And I fear a hopeless situation
Will become a treacherous path.

Or maybe I should trust myself,
And not place my hope
In a St Christopher
That was never really mine.

This is not

- ◯ A confession
- ◯ A weapon
- ◯ A guide
- ◯ A love letter
- ◯ The whole story
- ◯ An apology
- ◯ A response
- ◯ Reactionary
- ◯ Idealised
- ◯ For Annabelle Lee
- ◯ Wonderland
- ◯ For the bastard in the lions den
- ◯ Redemption
- ◯ Persuasion
- ◯ Shakespeare

Care.

And I said care;
That I care
When you were
Walking away.

You know those weren't
The four letters on my tongue.
But to wield words as a weapon?
That's not me.

Never will I wound another
By telling them
It's
Love.

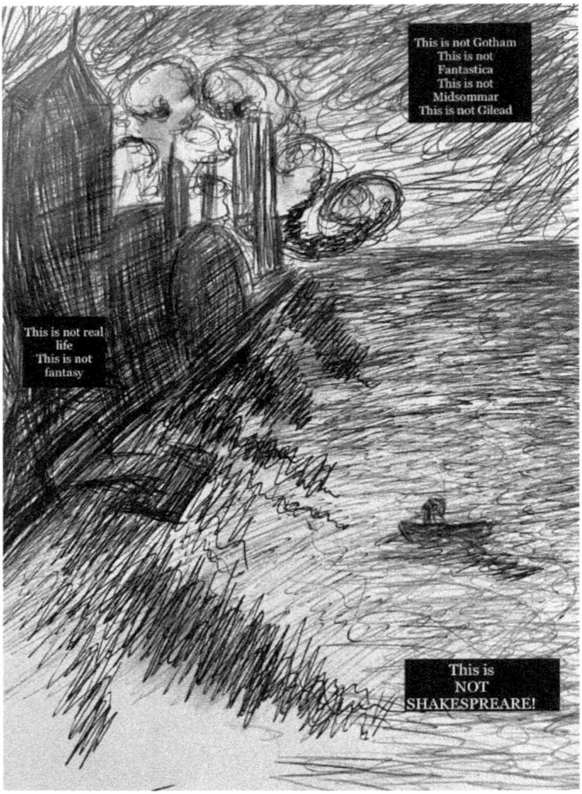
This is not Gotham
This is not
Fantastica
This is not
Midsommar
This is not Gilead
This is not real
life
This is not
fantasy
This is
NOT
SHAKESPREARE!

Scene 19

- ***Late Winter evening.***
- ***Car interior***
- ***Outside a storm builds.***
- ***'I'm Kissing You' by Des'ree plays on the radio.***
- ***A man argues with himself.***

1.T You should have said something.
1.M No, I didn't for a reason..
1.T But he knows. You should have said, he's..
1.M Yes, in a better place. But how would it help…
1.T What? That he is loved?
1.M I am an unnecessary complication. No I've done the right thing.
1.T Do you believe that?
[Music Builds: Where are you now?]
1.T Really, in your heart believe?
[Music Builds Louder: Where are you now?]
1.M This isn't a rom-com; I'm not Hugh Grant.
1.T So where are you going?
1.M I don't know. Back. I don;t know..
1.T Don't overthink it. Speak from the heart.

[Lights Dim. Foot steps. Door Bell]

[Spot light]

2.M Oh, hey, did you forget..

1.M Look, don't say anything. I need to say this, now, while I can. And I don't want you to say anything. I'm waiting. I have been waiting, everything I said before, I mean it. I care…

To Break The Crown.

'Heavy is the head';
No truer words were spoken
In a gallery of lost souls,
Faces from the past.
The nature of succession
And the precedent set before,
Makes the continuum of history,
Echo loud within these chambers.
Candles flicker,
Flames wax and wane
And the faces glance and dance
Inside their frame.
Should one reframe
These memories?
Set the ghosts in a context
More fitting?

(For the tales of the past are,
just that!
Tales of a time from before.)

Lovers from before
And their volumes
That line these halls,
Should no longer hold dominion,

Dictate the future
Of the one who sits atop the throne.
The blood and sweat of
Untold casualties,
The nights when the storms raged on,
When bodies lay waste in wreckage,
In a land that time forgot.
That the cost, while high,
Adds unnecessary weight
Upon the head it sits.

So,
Dismantle and displace the history
Which makes you feel inferior,
An imposter on a chair.
Smash the throne!
Shred the portraits!
Burn the volumes
That linger on dusted shelves!

Break the crown
And scatter the pieces,
And let a future
Grown anew.

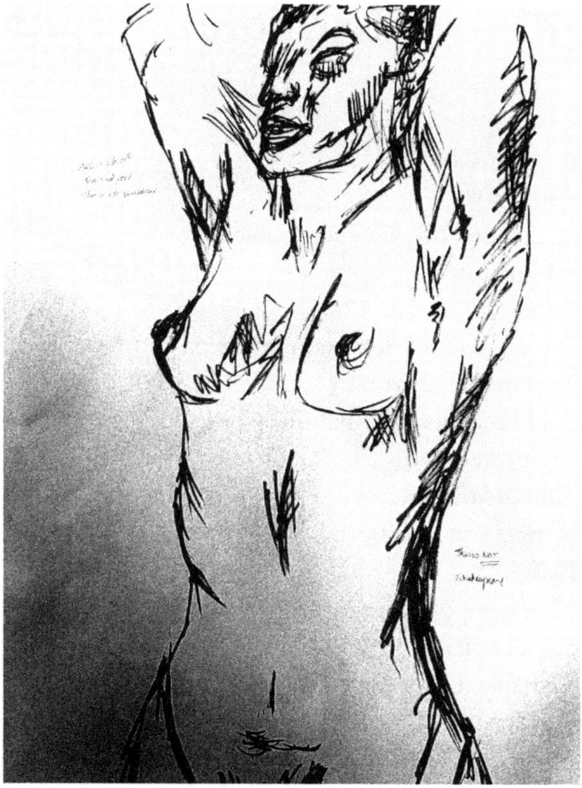

To Grieve.

It about what
Almost was.
A chance you allowed yourself
To imagine.
To say goodbye,
But never truly let the moment pass.
To expect the worst
And break as the final blow is struck.
Memories,
Albums of pictures
Where you will never
Be kept.
That tears of love,
Aren't wasted
Because it was for you.
For our time together,
A time when I was lost
Then found,
Found by you.
To know the last
Kiss was the last kiss.
That was I drowning before you,
And that last kiss pushed me
Beneath the surface
While giving me the means to breathe.

That I will grieve you grieve you
From afar,
And bury the words meant for you
In a message of obscurity,
That you might receive
A message in a bottle and reach for me?
That knowing you are in a better place
That you are ok,
That you can go on
Without me.

When I exist for you.

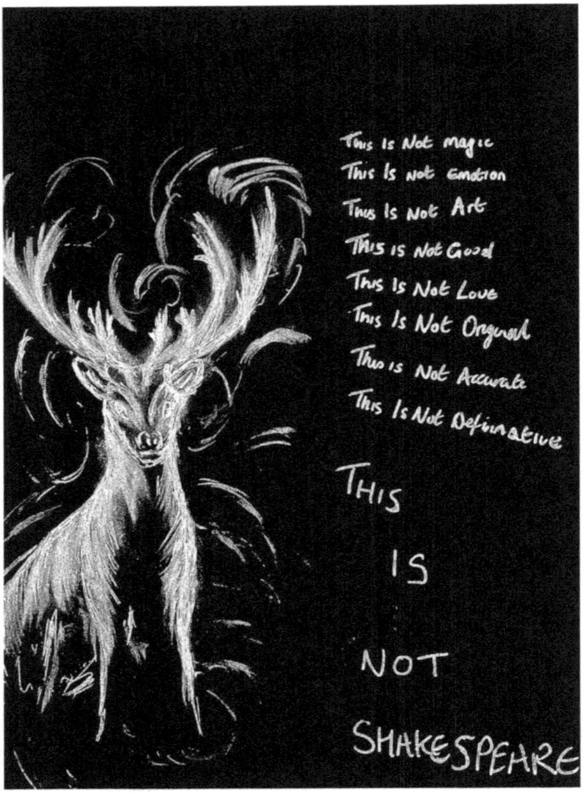
This Is Not magic
This Is not Emotion
This Is Not Art
This is Not Good
This Is Not Love
This Is Not Original
This is Not Accurate
This Is Not Definative
THIS
IS
NOT
SHAKESPEARE

Forgive.

There will always be 2 versions of events:
Different paths which
Brought us to different views
Of the same place.
I can't pretend to know
How you became who you are;
But I know my story
Is my truth.
I've taken the time to
Try to understand,
Attempted to heal
And one thing has become clear:
I will stay forever
In this comedy of errors
Haunted by a shadow.
Unless I take a step.

I'm sorry: I'm sorry
That I was not what you wanted,
How my faults weren't inline with
The vision you had.
I forgive you for breaking me
In an attempt to shape me into you ideal,
That your finger prints stay on my heart:
A heart that you tore apart.

I release you from responsibility,
The part you played in the person I became,
And rescind the power you hold
To keep me as a shell.
I wish you the best;
I hope you find happiness,
A love that you deserve, made for you
And a light that breaks your dark.

And I thank you;
For each lesson I learned,
The truth I discovered in myself
At a time when I was nothing.
This rebirth would not have been possible;
A well of strength not reached,
Had I not had the chance to reassemble
The pieces you pulled apart.
Pieces I now hold dear.

THIS IS NOT A BEST SELLER
Against the still
Azure expanse,
Spectres appear within my glance;
A Druidic herd
Without a word.
Shifting in the breeze,
Swift between the trees
A creeping shadow of birds.
THIS IS NOT SHAKESPEARE
Aa
"shadow"
shadows
shadowy
w e r t y u i o p

To Love.

Unashamed.
Unrestrained.
Unafraid.

Take hold of my hand and
Write with me;
Create stories, new chapters,
From the words you gave to me.

To love,
My love.

To love.

Just Coffee

It was just coffee;
That first cup was a a cup of understanding,
That began with a casual lack of expectation.
Finding an unexpected connection -
A cloth cut for the same pattern
Presented alongside steamed milk.

It was just coffee;
Recycled paper between my palms
As you explained the past and I understood
No more a revelation that a caveat;
The deeper notes to an intricate blend
Which made my cappuccino no less sweet.

It was just coffee;
The 6am caffeine boost to keep me going
The morning after I first stayed by your side.
No extra shot passed through a window
Could disrupt the dream
That turned day into night into day.

It was just coffee;
Thought it was latte for the hit,
You shot your shot - More.
With that, you cracked the weak spot in my shell
A coconut latte now the turning point,
As I left you entirely under my skin.

It was just coffee;
I choked down the cold and stagnant dregs
Forcing down the lump your words created;
In an instant the imitation of quality,
Not quite replicated by muddied salt water,
Left sitting at the bottom of what was once my
favorite mug.

It was just coffee;
Black and strong as my resolve
And bitter to swallow as I looked at you.
The expectation unwound,
At the proposition of another chance -
This time the Americano tender to the taste.

It was just coffee;
Freeze dried and sachetted and UHT cartons,
A necessity for a morning that followed
A night of fine and wine and a moment. That moment.
And a tingle on my lips from a chaste morning kiss
That lasted longer than a white cup morning buzz.

It was just coffee;
Cortana or Machiatto? The contents made irrelevant
By a looming overcast dulling the senses.
Burning on my tongue, as I approached too quick,
I stand before you scarred as a I promise -
Through the slow drip - I would wait for mist to clear.

It was just coffee;
As a storm whipped outside,
We spoke in caramel tones.
Warmed by the coffee machine glow -
The lightness of the aura shifting
As I set on my return to the night.

It was just coffee.
It was just coffee.
I swear it was just coffee.

It was never just coffee.

It was the first kiss.
It was the revelation.
It was the first morning after.
It was the request for more.
It was the text message breaking if off.
It was the conversation about trying again.
It was the taste of the last kiss
and not knowing it was the last.
It was giving up.
It was about giving hope.
It was books and jobs and music.
It was taking punt.
It was about crushing a good heart and walking away.

It was more than lattes and coconut milk.
It was more than instant granules and hotel kettles.
It was more than sugar free caramel and burnt beans.
It goes beyond the chocolate on a soya cappuccino .

It was never just coffee.
With you it was never just coffee.

And I will never drink coffee again.

Capture The Flag: The Pyre

A man sits beneath the moon on a crisp spring evening, pulling pages from the book of a mind long passed. The professions of love seemed juvenile against the backdrop of a the valley, made of peaks and drops he had traversed just recently. The way out may have been difficult, but the way back, following his time at a castle he could no longer see across the horizon.

The castle. The roses. The Red Queen.

These things seemed like a dream, but he still bore the scars of the journey back, of the vast hallways and empty chambers.The abandoned pennant.

He pulled the flag from beside his breast, the tattered remnant of the heart standard fluttering in the breeze as he unfurled it beneath the moonlight. Tonight, the night he returned to the safety of isolation, the man would out his sigil to rest. No longer will he stitch and patch and clamor to maintain a symbol that has been discarded and neglected.

Tonight, beneath the moonlight, with the words of a mind long passed, the man arranged a funeral pyre for the war torn flag.

And while it may be better to have loved and lost, the pages curled and the threads smoked, he watched the memories of a war torn heart turn to ash against the twilight air. Battle by battle, wound by wound.

Bittersweet and heartbreaking
Embers reaching for Orion.
By the rays of the new moon.

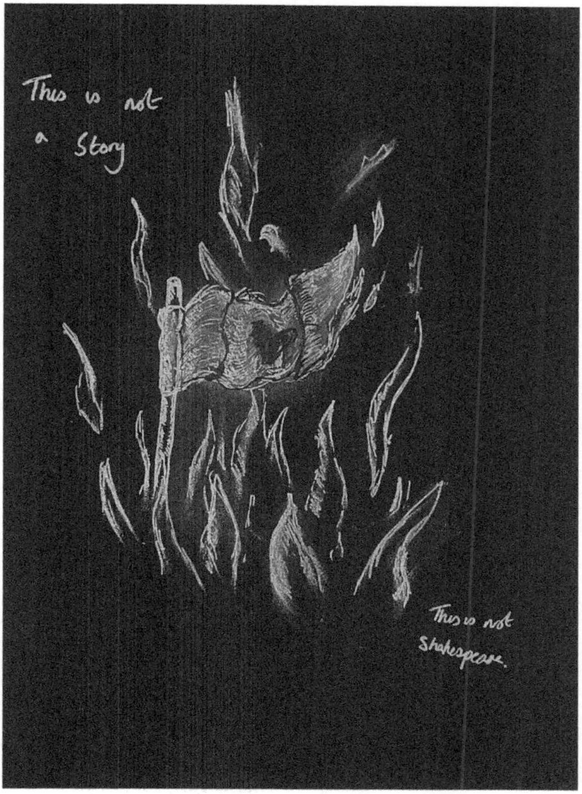
This is not
a Story
This is not
Shakespeare.

I Am Not An Imposter.

Maybe that's a bit of a contradiction.; finishing of the journey of discovering who I am but stating what I am not.

Firstly, I am thankful for everyone who has helped me get here. Man, Dad, Tom, Sarah, Fran, Arran, Steff, Leila, Evie and Conan(forever known as the 'Family Unit'). I don't make it easy to be around, but you guys have kept me alive.

You remind me that I am

- A son
- A brother
- An Uncle
- A Funcle
- A Guncle
- A friend
- Loved

Theres the usual suspects, anyone who has listened to me winging over another failed date, guy who didn't text back… Ry, Arran, Sam, Laura, Rhys, Sophie, Dyl, Kaz, Kris, Amy, Jayne, Luke, Shannon, Tom, Neil, John, all of PTOAS. Thank you for your support and advice and food.

From you I know I am

- Weird
- Funny
- Kind
- Creative
- Fun
- Loved

Theres the tribe of gays who have taken me in as one of their own; Jack, Karl, Alex, Phyll, Zak (honorary gay), Tyma, Neil, and the rest of the boys (The Vikings).

From you I have learnt I am

- Brave

- Nervous
- Determined
- Able
- Valued
- Appreciated
- Accepted
- Gay

And the work fam, who have to put up with some nonsense; Hannah, Laura, Sam, Amy, Amy, Hel, Jaz, Charlotte .

With you, I am

- Challenged
- Excited
- Silly
- Dramatic
- Part of a Team

A lot of credit in part goes to the creative influences in my life; Kelly Clarkson, Taylor Swift, Evanescence and Amy Lee, Dustin Kensure, Andrew Mcmahon, Kylie, Celine, Mariah, Christina, Muna, Britney, Florence, all the soundtrack to some of the biggest moments of my life.

Obviously big props to Shakespeare along with Matt Haig, Jeanette Winterson, Stephen King, Markus Zusak, Edgar Allan Poe, Joss Whedon, George R.R. Martin, Nathanial Hawthorn, H.P Lovecraft, Roahl Dahl, some of the amazing authors who have fuelled the fire of my imagination and gave me a place to hide when things got too much. (not forgetting Buffy the Vampire Slayer.)

The list of idiots who have challenged my worth. Thanks for showing me that I am

- Strong
- Worth so much more
- Resilient
- Kind
- Good
- Better without you.

<u>Mid Credits : Scene 28</u>

- ***Late Spring Afternoon.***
- ***Forrest***
- ***Above, birds sing in the trees.***
- ***'Lost In Paradise (Synthesis)' by Evanescence plays over earphones.***
- ***A man leans against a tree writing.***

1.M I feel like I can breathe.

To the man who challenged my thinking, whose fingerprints are all over these pages; Thank you. The moments within your sapphire gaze, though fleeting, are something I will never forget.

I Walk. I talk. I shop. I sneeze. I'm going to be a fireman when the floods roll back. There's trees in the desert since you moved out

And I don't sleep on a bed of bones.

Buffy Anne Summer
Buffy The Vampire Slayer
"Restless"
Season 4, Episode 22